HOW TO
RESPOND
—to—
DISASTER

Destiny Image Books by Bill Johnson

HOW TO

RESPOND

—— to ——

DISASTER

BY LIVING ANCHORED IN THE
GOODNESS OF GOD

BILL JOHNSON

DESTINY IMAGE® PUBLISHERS, INC.

PO Box 310, Shippensburg, PA 17257-0310

"Promoting Inspired Lives"

This book and all other Destiny Image and Destiny Image Fiction books are available at Christian bookstores and distributors worldwide.

Cover design by: Eileen Rockwell

For more information on foreign distributors, call 717-532-3040.

Or reach us on the Internet: www.destinyimage.com

ISBN 13 TP: 978-0-7684-5681-3

ISBN 13 EBook: 978-0-7684-5682-0

For Worldwide Distribution, Printed in the U.S.A.

1 2 3 4 5 6 / 23 22 21 20

Contents

Introduction

God is Good. This truth is the immovable bedrock of our faith, the cornerstone of theology, and the place from which we operate.

The following chapters have been excerpted from some of Pastor Bill Johnson's key teachings, providing believers anchors in times of fear, crisis, and uncertainty.

Rather than immediately dive into the "How To's" of responding to disaster, the first truth communicated so clearly is that we have the Father. And through Jesus we see clearly who He is and what our heavenly Father is like. *He is good!*

Then, in view of who God is, we respond—not react—to our present circumstances. From sickness to financial upheaval, from relationship struggles to global calamity, we discover everything in its rightful place when measured next to the character and nature of Father God, as revealed through Jesus. He has something to say about everything we are going through.

And what He says is always in line with who He is—God is good!

Enjoy this life-transforming, easy read and allow these words to stabilize your heart, no matter what is coming against you today. You have the Father—Jesus Christ reveals who He is. So, you have a Bible blueprint that *empowers you to handle everything that comes against you from a position of security, confidence, and victory*—because Jesus secured that victory for you!

Be settled and unshaken. Don't pretend away problems in the name of faith. Just simply refuse to exalt any crisis or disaster above the name of Jesus.

Larry Sparks
Publisher, Destiny Image

Chapter 1

We Have the Father

You must make your choice. Either this man was, and is, the Son of God, or else a madman or something worse. You can shut him up for a fool, you can spit at him and kill him as a demon or you can fall at his feet and call him Lord and God, but let us not come with any patronizing nonsense about his being a great human teacher. He has not left that open to us. He did not intend to.

—C.S. LEWIS, *Mere Christianity*

Why did Jesus become a man and come to earth? I realize that is a rather simple question understood by believers and sometimes by non-believers as well. Yet I wanted to find statements from Scripture answering this question. So years ago, I set out to read the New Testament in its entirety, looking for the answer to that one question—why did Jesus, the eternal Son of God, come to earth and become a man? Although I have misplaced the list derived from that study, here are a few of the passages and statements. We know:

1. Jesus came to atone for our sins. (See 1 John 2:2; 3:5.)

2. He came to take upon Himself the punishment that we deserved—our punishment in death. He then made it possible for us to receive what only He deserved—eternal life. (See Romans 5:6-11.)

3. He came to destroy the works of the evil one. (See 1 John 3:8.)

4. He came to make an open display of the foolishness of the devil and reveal the wisdom of the Cross. (See Colossians 2:15.)

5. He came that we might have abundant life. (See John 10:10.)

6. He came to initiate the present-tense awareness of the Kingdom of God—the realm and effects of God's rule. (See Matthew 6:10.)

7. Jesus came to save people's lives, not destroy
   them. (See Luke 9:56.)

This is not at all a comprehensive list. But it is
enough to illustrate my point. I had studied this subject
from cover to cover, yet I missed the primary reason for
His coming. *Jesus came to reveal the Father.* Every point
I had on my list was actually a sub-point to the primary
reason. Jesus came to a planet of orphans to reveal what
we needed most—Father God.

Tragically, that wonderful revelation suffers under
the broken condition of our present family culture.
Because so many have suffered under the abuse or
neglect of their biological fathers, the wonder of this
phenomenon is often lost. On the other hand, there's
never been a moment more ripe for this greatest
answer to human brokenness and need. Most of the
ills of humanity would be healed with that one revelation—Jesus came to set our focus, attention, and
affection on the Father, who is good. Our Father really
is perfect goodness.

> *Jesus came to a planet of orphans to reveal
> what we needed most—the Father.*

It wasn't that the goodness of God was missing in the Old Testament. In fact, that revelation of His goodness starts there: *"The Lord is good"* (Nahum 1:7 NASB). That revelation is laced throughout the Old Testament with His continual display of mercy toward a rebellious people. Time and time again, Israel brought disaster upon themselves through worshiping idols made by hands and giving themselves over to the sexual sins of the surrounding nations. Yet when they cried out to Him, He delivered them without complaint or punishment. His goodness drips from page after page of Scripture. Yet for some it gets lost in the midst of the wars, judgments, diseases, and disasters. When Jesus came, He made it nearly impossible to forget the new standard, as He brought a face to that goodness. It became personified in Him. Goodness became measurable—taste worthy. (See Psalm 34:8.)

Both the mystery and the revelation of God's goodness are contained in Jesus. In reading through the Gospel of John—the Gospel that contains the bulk of the revelation of why Jesus came to earth—we find that when we see Jesus, we see the Father. (See John 14:9.) We then discover that He says only what the Father is saying. (See John 12:49-50.) We also come to realize that Jesus does only what the Father is doing. (See John 5:19.) And so everything that we love and admire about Jesus is actually a precise and calculated manifestation of the Father. God is *the* Father, and the Father is good.

> *Throughout our history, God has spoken to our ancestors by His prophets in many different ways. The revelation He gave them was only a fragment at a time, building one truth upon another. But to us living in these last days, God now speaks to us openly in the language of a Son, the appointed Heir of everything, for through Jesus God created the panorama of all things and all time. The Son is the dazzling radiance of God's splendor, the exact expression of God's true nature—his mirror image!* (Hebrews 1:1-3 The Passion Translation)

This is a stunning section of Scripture. It tells us that Jesus is the exact representation of the Father—His nature and His person. He emanates from the Father's being, manifesting His glory (remember goodness,

Exodus 33:18-19). It's interesting to note that when Jesus informed the disciples that He was going back to the Father, and that He would send the Comforter—the Holy Spirit—He used a very specific word: *"I will ask the Father, and He will give you **another** Helper, that He may be with you forever"* (John 14:16 NASB). The word used here for "another" means *one that is exactly the same*. Let me illustrate.

As I write this book, I'm looking at the furniture in my living room. There are two couches facing each other in front of a fireplace. They are exactly the same—mirror images of each other. We have another couch in our family room, but its color, shape, and size are quite a bit different from the two in our living room. I could accurately say, "I have another couch in my family room." But I couldn't use the word used in John 14, because while my family room couch qualifies as a couch, it isn't exactly the same as the two in my living room.

What's the point? When we look at Jesus, He is **exactly** the same as His Father. Then Jesus sent the Holy Spirit, who is **exactly** like Jesus. In other words,

God wanted to make sure that there would be no chance of missing the revelation needed to permeate and shift the course of history at this point and time— the revelation of our God as a good and perfect Father.

Jesus reveals a Father who is not abusive or self-serving. The Holy Spirit, who now lives in us, reaffirms the wonder and beauty of this perfectly good Father. The work that He is doing in us is all about deepening our connection to the Father, who brings identity, purpose, destiny, and an awareness of unlimited resources to accomplish our purpose in life. When the Holy Spirit is able to do His perfect work in us, our connection to all that is good is strengthened and made clear. This revelation of God as our Father is the ultimate expression of the goodness of God.

The Beauty of Discipline

When I talk about this perfect Father, I'm not talking about someone who refuses to discipline His children. And while the subject of discipline is not what people want to hear, it is real and needed. The truth of the matter is that He loves us too much to leave us as we are. Some of the most significant changes only take place in that context. According to Scripture, discipline proves we belong to Him as sons and daughters. (See Hebrews 12:7-8.) Those who are without discipline are not real heirs and descendants. They are fakes. They may talk the talk, but you can't authentically walk the walk without discipline.

When Beni and I were raising our children, we determined to make discipline an event, not an impulsive outburst. Outbursts are for the sake of the parent, not the child. "That child crossed my will, and I'll show him who is boss." And so the physically larger person yells or gives a swat. In a strange way it makes the parent feel vindicated, and that he or she is at least trying to keep that child from becoming an uncontrollable detriment to society. We all want to be good caregivers to our children.

Beni and I purposed to never discipline our children out of anger. Outbursts and anger had nothing to do with a loving concern for a child. Giving a swat on the butt or a verbal outburst does little to shape a child's heart in the right way. Impulsive reactions undermine our intent. Discipline then becomes a release valve for the parent, and has little to do with the well-being or the forming of the child's heart. Changing the focus changes the method, which changes the outcome.

Our policy was, before there was discipline of any kind, I sent the child to his or her room so that I could take whatever time needed to prepare my heart. I had to make sure I was going in the room for the child's sake, and not mine. I had to be firm, but not angry; compassionate, but not careless. Interestingly, the child that was disciplined usually wanted to spend the rest of the evening with me, on my lap, or playing a game with me. Done correctly, discipline serves and, strangely, unites. It doesn't divide.

Jesus talked about this in John 15. This is the chapter on the vine, the vinedresser, and the fruit. To illustrate discipline, Jesus talks about pruning. God rewards all growth with pruning. It doesn't happen only when there's something wrong. It's that, left untended, vines will grow to a place where they bear little to no fruit. All the energy of the vine goes into growing branches and leaves. God is very concerned with fruit from our lives and does whatever is needed to keep that priority in place.

If we are left unchecked, our growth is in appearance (religious—form without power). And just as Adam and Eve covered themselves with leaves to hide their nakedness, so we hide our immaturity behind the appearance of growth and not in the substance of Christlikeness. There is to be fruit of being like Jesus—converts, miracles, answers to prayer, and a changed life. Jesus said:

> *"I am the true vine, and My Father is the vinedresser. Every branch in Me that does not bear fruit, He takes away; and every branch that bears fruit, He prunes it so that it may bear more fruit. You are already clean because of the word which I have spoken to you"* (John 15:1-3 NASB).

I find this passage very interesting. Jesus lets them know there will be pruning in their lives. But Jesus follows the statement with *"You are already clean because of the word which I have spoken to you."* The word for clean is the same basic word as *prune*. And our becoming clean (disciplined) in this context happens through His Word and/or His voice. Think about it—pruning/discipline, takes place when He talks to us. That is amazing.

I grew up thinking that bad circumstances in my life were His discipline. That is inconsistent with the lesson given by Jesus to His disciples. Since then I've learned that oftentimes the bad circumstances are brought on by us, but they serve to turn us back to a place of listening. The large fish that swallowed Jonah wasn't the discipline of the Lord. He ran into that "wall" running from God (the Voice). But the fish helped bring Jonah back to the place of wanting to hear from God.

I'm not saying that circumstances can never be part of discipline. I'm just saying that even then, He simply wants to talk to us to bring about the change in us that is needed. A lot happens when He talks and we listen from the heart, thus becoming the doers of His Word as He always intended. (See James 1:21.)

Jesus Disciplines His Disciples

Luke chapter 9 is one of the more interesting and entertaining chapters in the Bible. It's worthy of great study. This chapter is my favorite in seeing how Jesus dealt with His disciples when they were doing and saying stupid things. Jesus had made these guys very powerful, and now they are doing things that are very inconsistent with the standard that Jesus set for Himself and for them.

This is the chapter where the twelve are given power and authority to minister in Jesus' name (verse 2) and are then sent out in pairs to their hometowns to preach the Gospel of the Kingdom (see Luke 9:6). When they return, they meet with Jesus to let Him know what they said and did. There is obvious excitement, as they did what Jesus did without Him being there. Miracles took place through their words and hands. Jesus later let them know that their real celebration had to be in the fact their names are written in Heaven (see Luke 10:20).

Following their time of great ministry success, strange things began to surface. The first was they began to argue as to who was the greatest. I can only imagine that they began to think this way because of the miracles that flowed through them. Remember, they were sent out two by two, which means there were ten other disciples who were not present when the powerful things happened through them. In their minds it might have been hard for them to imagine that the other disciples experienced things that were quite as significant as what they experienced.

Jesus, knowing what they were talking about, realized it was time to prune a branch. If their concept of greatness was based on the miracles that flowed through them, they were in trouble. If that *branch* were allowed to grow, it would remove all possibility of lasting fruit for the glory of God. And so Jesus pointed to a child, and let them know what real greatness in the Kingdom looked like. He said, "...*For it is the one who is least among you all who is the greatest*" (Luke 9:48 NIV). Jesus introduced them once again to the mystery of His Kingdom, where we gain by giving and rise by going low.

As soon as Jesus addressed their preoccupation with personal greatness, the disciples made another blunder. They saw someone trying to cast out demons in Jesus' name. So they rebuked him, trying to maintain their franchise on Kingdom power. It's almost like they're saying, "Okay. We get it. We're not better than each other. But we are certainly better than him!" Because they had the access to Jesus that no one else had, they took that on as a measure of personal accomplishment, instead of personal responsibility, as in *"to whom much is given, much is required"* (see Luke 12:48). They missed it.

Once again Jesus spoke to them life-changing words: *"Do not hinder him; for he who is not against you is for you"* (Luke 9:50 NASB). I remind you, Jesus is bringing discipline to the twelve, pruning back a branch that would not bear fruit in the future if it continued to develop in the direction it is going. The idea of elitism would cost them greatly in the future if it was not addressed now. They also needed to know that some of their support would come from people who are not in their club. As stated in John 15:3, this process of His word spoken to them is what is making them clean, pruned. Issues of the heart are always addressed with Jesus talks. Receiving that word changes us. (See James 1:21.)

That was not the end. The problems of their hearts seemed only to increase and rise to the surface in the most inopportune times. Remember, this chapter is the record of the great experiment—giving power to very imperfect disciples. In the very next scene, James and John want to call down fire upon an entire city because they rejected their ministry. The spirit of murder is now functioning through the disciples to the point that they actually want to kill the citizens of an entire city. Obviously the heart to murder is wrong. But the need to be vindicated in order to feel good about ourselves is very shaky ground to build upon. This branch—thought, belief, and idea—had to be dealt with through discipline.

The Day of Judgment is in His hands. The day of mercy is in ours.

As a side note, what kinds of things did they see God do through their ministries on their recent missionary journey that would make them think that with

Jesus' approval they could actually pull this off—call down fire from Heaven? If this branch were allowed to grow, it could threaten the very purpose of the vine entirely. Jesus exposes their hearts with a word: *"You do not know what kind of spirit you are of; for the Son of Man did not come to destroy men's lives, but to save them"* (Luke 9:55-56 NASB). The New King James Version of this story emphasizes that they used Elijah as an example for what they were asking. *"Lord, do You want us to command fire to come down from heaven and consume them, just as Elijah did?"* (Luke 9:54). I think it's funny how often we find a verse to justify what we know in our hearts to be wrong. The disciples had already witnessed Jesus' approach to people and knew that His heart was one of great compassion and mercy.

It's also interesting to note that to call down fire was perfect in Elijah's day but was now very wrong in Jesus' day. Elijah perfectly fulfilled his assignment. But his assignment wasn't to reveal the Father. Jesus, knowing that such an action would undermine the revelation of the Father, told His disciples that they would have to be empowered by a different spirit to carry out that plan of calling down fire upon a city.

He then listed another reason for His coming—to save people's lives, not destroy them. I wish more people would get this. I once had a lady curse and rebuke me and actually try to cast a demon out of me at the back door of the sanctuary for not agreeing with her in prayer for the destruction of San Francisco. Thankfully the only devil present left when she did. I had her kindly escorted to the exit.

Don't get me wrong, the sins of that city, and most others, are great. Inexcusable? Yes. Unforgiveable? No. This isn't the Day of Judgment. This is the day of great mercy. The Day of Judgment is in His hands. The day of mercy is in ours. All of us who received His forgiveness have done so because of His mercy. All we're praying is, "God, I know I'm no better than the people of this city. Please show them the same undeserved mercy You've shown to me."

God longs to extend His mercy to people who no longer recognize the difference between their right hand and their left. (See Jonah 4:11.) That is not a derogatory remark about their intelligence. Far from it. It's a statement about the ability of the majority to distinguish between right and wrong. This is a day when insanity is called sanity, wrong is considered right, and foolishness is called nobility. Babies are murdered in the name of *rights*, while animals are protected in the name of *responsibilities*. And all this is fought for with an *offering* of zeal that God alone is worthy of receiving. We are in desperate need of His mercy upon our cities and nations.

Luke 9 records the great experiment in which Jesus entrusts His power and authority to twelve men who really aren't that stable or mature. The very fact that they would argue about who is the greatest, and want to restrict the activities of all who don't belong to their group, and then follow it up with attempted murder should let us know the condition of these men. I can assure you, if I had one of my pastoral staff members confide in me that he was asked to leave a city because his ministry was rejected, and now he had a plan to blow up the entire community, I would be greatly concerned about his place in ministry. I'd at least restrict his activities and have him get help.

Jesus doesn't even seem surprised when these issues come up. And in every case He has a specific word of correction and redirection. But nowhere does He lose His temper. Nowhere does He punish them and make them "sit on the bench" while the others continue following Him. He spoke, and they were changed. And these issues never came up again.

> *Graveyards are orderly and clean. Nurseries filled with babies are not. One is alive, and the other is dead. If you want increase, get a shovel, and learn how to patiently work with people who are in process.*

The Funniest Surprise of All!

Many would consider entrusting authority and power to the twelve disciples to be a failed experiment. Apparently Jesus doesn't, as He then does the unexplainable—He follows this experiment by entrusting this same power and authority to seventy others, releasing them into the same kind of ministry as the twelve. *"Now after this the Lord appointed seventy others, and sent them in pairs ahead of Him to every city and place where He Himself was going to come"* (Luke 10:1

NASB). That is astonishing. Apparently, Jesus is not as afraid of messes as we are.

One of my favorite ministry verses in the Bible is in Proverbs 14:4: *"Where no oxen are, the manger is clean, but much revenue comes by the strength of the ox."* The goal of many in ministry is no messes. And that becomes the measure of success. I remind you, graveyards are orderly and clean. Nurseries filled with babies are not. One is alive, and the other is dead. If you want increase, get a shovel, and learn how to patiently work with people who are in process.

Jesus reveals the Father as perfectly good. He revealed Him in every word (teaching) and action (miracles and acts of kindness). He then gives us the Holy Spirit to emulate Him through us. There's to be no mistake or let down in the ongoing revelation of what the Father is like. It is to happen through us as it happened through Jesus.

Secrets to Saving Sin-Filled Cities

Many want to curse sinners, but that curse is a misuse of authority and purpose. God calls us priests of the Lord (see 1 Peter 2:9). In priestly ministry we represent people before God and God before people. Representing people before God is a prayer-type ministry, often called intercession. The task at hand is to stand in the gap—the place of obvious breakdown in spiritual equilibrium and values—and pray for mercy on their behalf. (See Ezekiel 22:30.) Someone did that for us. We must now do it for others.

Tragically, in the Ezekiel passage mentioned, God couldn't find anyone who would cry out for mercy for those in need. To take our God-given assignment to pray on behalf of someone and turn that moment into a curse is a complete misuse of a God-given responsibility. Giving an account to God for the misuse of that assignment is going to sting. This might be part of the reason why the Bible says He will wipe away our tears.

God longs for us to co-labor with Him. Intercessory prayer is such a role. And so is the lifestyle of miracles. Jesus brought a rebuke to three cities because they had seen His ongoing life of miracles (see Matthew 11:20-24). While they applauded His works, they didn't adjust their lifestyle to this standard that was now being revealed to them. In other words, they didn't repent. To *repent* basically means "to change our way of thinking." So the miracles they saw didn't change how they thought or how they saw their responsibilities in life. Jesus then made a shocking conclusion: *"If the miracles had occurred in Sodom which occurred in you, it would have remained to this day"* (Matthew 11:23 NASB). Do you see it? If a ministry like Jesus' ministry were to have happened in the city of Sodom, the city known by the judgment of God released over it, it would still be here. Sodom would have repented! Miracles, in the measure that Jesus demonstrated, will turn a Sodom from a city of judgment to a city of purpose with great legacy and endurance. Their lost-ness makes purpose and destiny easy to recognize. Religious cities, in the sense of form without power, are insulated from realizing their need for God and the direction He brings.

God longs to show mercy. But when people partner with one another to curse a city, or a celebrity, a politician, an evil boss, etc., we are violating the reason we're alive. He looks for those who will stand in the gap with intercession. Why? Because He is good! And without people standing in the gap, interceding for those needing mercy, the manifestation of His goodness will be missed.

This Changes Everything

Everything He said and did worked to fulfill that one assignment—reveal the Father. When I realized that simple point, it changed everything. It created a context and, more importantly, a reason for every word and action of Jesus. The Father was to be made known to this planet of orphans.

When Jesus responded to the cry of blind Bartimaeus, He was representing the Father. There's not one of us, if we had the ability to turn our blind child into a seeing child, who wouldn't do it. It's what fathers do. We fix things. And in this case, Jesus took care of Bartimaeus' blindness by opening his eyes, but He also gave him a new identity. The blind man threw aside his beggar's garment when he came to Jesus. That garment was his badge of employment, given by the priests, to prove he was deserving of alms.

When they brought the woman caught in adultery to Jesus to see what He would do, He once again represented the Father. The religious leaders brought stones to kill her according to the Law they lived under. But Jesus came with a different assignment. He bent over and wrote in the dirt, telling those intending to stone her to go ahead, under this condition: *"Let any one of you who is without sin be the first to throw a stone at her"* (John 8:7 NIV). Interestingly, the only one without sin refused to cast a stone at all. Instead, He revealed the Father. In reality, this was a Father-daughter moment.

All those intending to stone her to death fled the scene. Whatever Jesus wrote released such an atmosphere of grace that those driven by judgment had to leave. Jesus then did what any one of us would have done if our daughter were lost in such moral failure and humiliating shame. He served her. Jesus didn't care what the religious leaders thought of Him. The opinions of the crowd didn't matter either. The Father had to be seen. And more importantly, the Father had to be known by this one who was lost, this one who was manifesting her orphaned heart.

In the Old Covenant she would have been stoned to death. But this is a different season, even though the Old Covenant was still in play, as the blood of Jesus had not been shed yet. Her sin wasn't ignored or treated lightly. Once she acknowledged that her accusers had left and there was now no one to condemn her, Jesus said, *"Neither do I condemn you. Go and sin no more"* (John 8:11 NKJV). He disciplined her—with loving words.

Every action and every word pointed to the perfect Father, the One who is completely good. When the disciples thought children were not quite as important as the adults Jesus was ministering to, Jesus corrected them. Children flock around good dads. On top of that, parents entrust their children to good dads. Jesus simply illustrated this phenomenon that took the disciples a while to catch on to. He was manifesting the Father to people, and the children saw it before most.

> *And they were bringing children to Him so that He might touch them; but the disciples rebuked them. But when Jesus saw this, He was indignant and said to them, "Permit the children to*

come to Me; do not hinder them; for the kingdom of God belongs to such as these" (Mark 10:13-14 NASB).

Page after page, story after story shows how Jesus revealed the Father in word and deed. The priestly prayer of Jesus in John 17 opens for us some of the most intimate moments between Jesus and His Father. To me it sounds like Jesus is giving an account of how He spent His time on planet Earth to His Father. The entire chapter is worth reading just for this single purpose—how did Jesus give an account of His life on earth? Just seeing this helps us to see the understanding that Jesus had in what He was to do in coming to this planet. Jesus mentions many things in His prayer, but there are four things I'd like to list from this great chapter of John 17:

1. 1. I have finished the work (verse 4).

2. I have manifested Your name (verse 6).

3. I have given them Your word (verse 14).

4. I have declared Your name (verse 26).

Jesus Reviews His Assignment Before the Father

1. *Jesus came to finish the work of the Father.*
   Remember, it's the family business that Jesus
   continued in, touching and healing people's
   lives. *"If I do not do the works of My Father, do not
   believe Me"* (John 10:37 NASB). Encountering
   the work of the Father introduces that person
   to the Father Himself. "Believe the works, that
   you may know and believe that the Father is in
   Me, and I in Him" (John 10:38 NKJV). That
   has been the nature and heart of God from day
   one. But it was never fully realized until Jesus.

2. *Jesus was a manifestation of the name of the
   Father.* Names reveal nature and identity.
   Jesus revealed the nature and identity of the
   Father. He lived in complete harmony with the
   name of the Father, confessing that He came
   in His name. (See John 5:43.) The miracles
   that Jesus performs are done in His Father's
   name. (See John 10:25.) The right and authority to become children of God was given to

those who believe in His name, as He came in the name of His Father. (See John 1:12.)

3. ***Jesus gave people the word of the Father.*** Jesus was revealed as the Word of God. (See John 1:1.) He was described as the Word made flesh. (See John 1:14.) He only said what the Father was saying. He also said that those who hear His word and believe have eternal life. (See John 5:24.) Jesus then identifies the Source of the word He spoke: *"If anyone loves Me, he will keep My word; and My Father will love him, and We will come to him and make Our home with him. He who does not love Me does not keep My words; and the word which you hear is not Mine but the Father's who sent Me"* (John 14:23-24 NKJV). Remember that the worlds were created by the word of God. Whenever He spoke, things were created. It's the same today. Saying what God is saying is one of the things we can do to release His life, love, and presence into the world around us.

4. ***Jesus declared His name.*** He already mentioned that He manifested His name. But now Jesus emphasizes that the name of the Father was also something that had to be declared. Some things must be proclaimed to have full effect. Jesus is the declaration from Heaven as to who this Father is—He is exactly like Jesus! Page after page of the Gospels we see Jesus declaring that all He said and did came from His Father. He took none of the glory for Himself, but instead made it known that He was merely declaring what had to be said.

Saying what God is saying is one of the things we can do to release His life, love, and presence into the world around us.

It's a Clear Assignment

On several occasions Beni and I have had foster children live with us for a season. On one of the more tragic occasions, we had two boys given to us whose parents had killed themselves. First it was the mom, because of abuse; and then, perhaps about six months later, the dad. Thankfully after a few weeks in our home their counselors said they didn't need counseling anymore. The children knew we loved them and they began to experience peace of heart and mind. But the first night or two in our home was quite interesting.

When it came time to eat dinner, they grabbed all the food they could reach and wrapped their arms around their plates so that no one else could take it. They showed us how orphans live. We smiled and assured them they could have all they wanted, and that there would be more than enough again tomorrow. It took a little while, but soon they learned that provision was assured because they now lived with us.

Orphans live differently from children who know they're loved. Self-preservation and self-promotion are not the driving points of the behavior of healthy children. Instead the secure child is more inclined to celebrate the gift of another without fighting for the attention. All around us are orphans. It doesn't matter if we're talking about our neighbors, our bosses, our friends in church, the conflict in the Middle East, or even the battle between political parties—we are being led and fed by orphans. They have no answers. They just have different ways of deadening the pain.

People of God, now is the time to rise up. We have the privilege to know this wonderful Father for ourselves and deal once and for all with the part of us that wants to hoard all the food on our plates. And from our personal victory we have the privilege to make Him known, giving the chance for others to experience Him for themselves.

Jesus gave the following assignment to His disciples: *"As the Father has sent Me, I also send you"* (John 20:21 NASB). Hopefully you can see by now that the assignment given to Jesus was to reveal the Father. In this passage Jesus passes on this part of His assignment to us; and in doing so, He defines our purpose in much the same way as His. We still live in a world that He loves. This world is filled with people who will never really know their right hand from their left. The perspective on the values of Heaven only really comes to those who know the Father—and that the Father is good.

Chapter 2

Jesus Christ, Perfect Theology

I still have questions for God…absolutely. But it is within faith, not outside faith, and surely not opposed to faith.

—ELI WIESEL

There is a deep, personal need in the Body of Christ to see Jesus for who He is. Jesus Christ is perfect in every way. He is perfect beauty, perfect majesty, perfect power, and perfect humility. The list of His wonderful characteristics and virtues is endless. But for the sake of this chapter, Jesus Christ is perfect theology—He is the will of God personified.

Jesus' Response to Problems

Jesus healed all who came to Him, no exceptions. He also healed all the Father directed Him to heal.

Setting another standard than what Jesus gave us is unacceptable.

Jesus stilled every life-threatening storm that He encountered. We never see Him using His authority to increase the impact of a storm or to bring calamity of any kind. Never once did He command the storm to destroy a city so that its citizens would become more humble and learn to pray, thus becoming more like Him.

Today, many of our spiritual leaders announce why God sent the storm—to break the pride and sinfulness of a region. Obviously God can use any tragedy to His purposes. But that doesn't mean the problem was His design. Jesus didn't deal with storms in that way. Regardless of how or why the storm came about, Jesus was the solution. In our world many insurance companies and newspapers call natural disasters "acts of God." Perhaps they got their theology from us.

By thinking that God causes our storms, diseases, and conflicts, are we resorting to the same reasoning as did James and John when they said, *"as Elijah did"*? (See Luke 9:54.) They justified their thinking by using an Old Testament standard for a New Testament dilemma. Are we truly justified for having such a response because we can find a biblical precedent in the Old Testament?

> ***Whatever you think you know about God that you can't find in the person of Jesus you have reason to question. Jesus Christ is the fullest and most precise revelation of the Father and His nature that could ever be made known.***

Why did Jesus rebuke the storm instead of just telling it to stop? The implication is that the powers of darkness were involved in the storm, and they needed to be dealt with because they violated the heart and purpose of God on the earth. And if the devil is involved in the storm, we don't want to be found saying the storm is the will of the Father.

Deliverance came to all who asked. This is Jesus. He illustrated this when the Syrophoenician woman came to Him on behalf of her daughter. (See Mark 7:24-30.) Jesus wasn't supposed to minister to her because she was a Gentile—His ministry was first to be offered to the Jew to fulfill the mandate of Scripture. This was a necessary step in order to open up the Gospel to every nation. Yet even here we see Jesus moved with the heart of compassion for people. He brought deliverance/healing to this young lady as a manifestation of the Father to a girl in need. Once again, Jesus revealed the Father exactly. And as a reminder, this is the work of the Holy Spirit upon Jesus, who lives in us to manifest the same.

Whatever you think you know about God that you can't find in the person of Jesus you have reason to question. Jesus Christ is the fullest and most precise revelation of the Father and His nature that could ever be made known.

There is a vast difference between the goodness of God seen in the life of Jesus and the goodness of God revealed through the belief system of the average church in the Western world. It has become easier for us to believe that either the standard Jesus set for our lives is metaphorical and therefore entirely unattainable for today or that it is theologically wrong to consider Jesus' example as a legitimate standard—it is historical only.

At the root of the confusion is the difficulty in reconciling the differences in the life of Jesus and the experience of the everyday believer. To cover the discrepancies we often create theology that keeps us comfortable, but also locked in perpetual immaturity. It has been easier to change our interpretation of Scripture by finding out why something didn't happen than it is to seek God until He answers with power.

> *It's not that our belief systems change God. Our belief systems, or in this case unbelief systems, limit the activities of God in our lives.*

Jesus' Response to Disease

If Jesus healed everyone who came to Him, and the Father wills for people to be sick, then we have a divided house—one that, according to the teachings of Jesus, cannot stand. Invariably it's at this point in the discussion that Old Testament verses are brought up in an attempt to prove that God causes the very things I suggest we are to bring answers to, i.e., sickness, storms, torment, etc. And then we're told, "God changes not!" It's strange to me that this statement is used to prove God continues to cause sickness but not to prove that, in the same way, Jesus healed everyone who came to Him. This is tragic because it is in His heart for us to do the same. It is true that God doesn't change. It's now important for us to see that He was the Merciful One in the Old as well as the New Testament. It just wasn't until Jesus came that we got to see clearly what the Father was like.

We must ask ourselves how much of the Old Covenant we want preserve. Is it a legitimate endeavor to preserve the standard of a God that causes our problems? Whatever we preserve is what we'll have to live under. It's not that our belief systems change God. Our belief systems, or in this case unbelief systems, limit the activities of God in our lives. There are severe warnings in Scripture about limiting God. *"How often they provoked Him in the wilderness, and grieved Him in the desert! Yes, again and again they tempted God, and limited the Holy One of Israel. They did not remember His power: the day when He redeemed them from the enemy"* (Psalm 78:40-42 NKJV).

There are very few areas of the Christian life that the Church is willing to compromise on in this way, other than miracles, signs, and wonders. For example, we would never tell people to sacrifice sheep to atone for their sins. Jesus did that once and for all. Neither would we make people travel to Jerusalem so they can be involved in acceptable worship to God. Jesus taught that present-day worship is not in a place, but is in Spirit and truth (see John 4:21-24). We would never think of forbidding those with physical deformities from coming before His presence in worship (see Leviticus 21:18-21). Nor would we ever consider the blind as cursed by God (see Deuteronomy 28:28). We will faithfully pray for the rebellious teenager, but we'd never stone that young person to death (see Deuteronomy 21:18-21).

Yet each of these statements represents God's dealings with people under the Old Covenant. Is it then not also true that these dealings with man reveal God's nature—one that changes not? God nearly killed Moses because he had not circumcised his sons. Yet for us it is optional. We are now told to love our enemies, while in the Old Testament God commanded Israel to kill the enemy nations—every man, woman, and child. Elijah had eight hundred demon-possessed devil worshipers killed, yet Jesus gave Himself up for execution in the place of the wicked. Is it legal to continue to embrace those standards when Jesus came to reveal the Father more accurately?

But historically the Church has done this very thing with the subjects of healing and deliverance. If an Old Testament Scripture supersedes the perfect revelation of God found in Jesus Christ in the area of healing, then it also has that right in this list given above. Once again, we don't do this with any other part of the Gospel than we do with the realm of miracles, signs, and wonders. It is a present-day phenomenon—it has not always been this way.

It astounds me that the effort to be like Jesus can be so controversial. And strangely the opposition comes from those who confess Christ. In this day when people say we're to become Christ-like, they mean that we're to be patient, kind, loving, etc. The purity part of life is essential to being a faithful witness. But the power aspect is equal in importance. Purity and power are the two legs we stand on in giving witness to the resurrection of Jesus Christ, which is what we are witnesses of—the resurrection.

Two thousand years ago, all sickness was considered to be from the devil, and healing was from God—a sign of the present reality of God's Kingdom. Even something as simple as a fever was considered to be of the devil (see Mark 1:31). Things have disintegrated so far that many consider sickness to be sent or allowed by God to build our character, while those who pursue the ministry of healing are thought to be out of balance at best, and from the devil at worst. This is especially true if that person believes that everyone is to be healed. It's frightening to see how far things can fall in two thousand years.

What is even more puzzling is that the very ones who consider the sickness to be approved or even sent by God for our benefit have no problem going to the doctor to find a cure and release from disease. Such mindless approaches to Scripture must stop. And those who would never receive prayer for healing consider going to the doctor common sense. It may be common, but it lacks sense when it violates the example given to us in Scripture. Sometimes when we lack the experience mentioned in Scripture, we tend to look for an obscure passage that somehow explains and/or excuses our lack of experience in the place of the overwhelming evidence given through the life of Jesus.

For what it's worth, I have no problem with going to doctors or taking medicine. They can be used by God to bring about the intended result—health. You just can't have it both ways—believe that God sent a disease to teach us and then try to get rid of it through medical intervention. If that is your belief, you are violating the sovereignty of God. I do have a concern that so many live under the influence of "modern medicine" and give little or no thought to going to the Great Physician. I pray for healing but am willing to accept medical assistance, and I personally do that without shame.

As perfect theology, Jesus illustrates the will of God. He models how life is to be lived modeling the reality of His Kingdom.

Consider this: many have been trained to embrace disease as a form of suffering for which we gain favor with God. If we can legitimately do that with sickness, we can do it with sin. Jesus paid the same price to render both realities powerless—see Psalm 103:3, Isaiah 33:24, Mark 2:9, and James 5:16.

Jesus Christ, Perfect Theology

Jesus Christ, the Model for Life

As perfect theology, Jesus illustrates the will of God. He models how life is to be lived modeling the reality of His Kingdom. In this Kingdom, you live by dying, rise by going low, and receive by giving. The list of these logical contradictions seems endless. Yet they profoundly reveal His Kingdom—His heart. Below is a handful of areas that modeled how life is to be lived as it pertains to:

Possessions—Jesus illustrates the heart of the Father in everything He says and does. He models our approach to possessions. I remind you He is God. He owns everything in Heaven and on earth. But His love is measured by what He gave—Himself. Jack Hayford defined abundance as being measured in what I've given away, not by what I have. Brilliant. Jesus modeled His value for excellence in wearing a seamless robe but kept a priority on caring for the poor and standing up for those who had no voice. Both Old and New Testament illustrate that obedience can make a person prosperous. But Jesus brought a warning not often recognized in the Old—true riches, which are the unseen realities of

51

the Kingdom for here and now, are better than money. And the love of money can cost us true riches.

Economics—Jesus illustrated the beauty of giving as the priority of the Kingdom finances. He also taught the power of contentment, knowing the lust for possessions is a cancer of the soul. But many make the mistake of thinking Jesus to be a socialist. Nothing could be further from the truth. He promises that for the disciples who left all to follow Him, they would receive one hundred times what they left—now, in this lifetime. (See Mark 10:28-30.) In His parables of the talents and minas (see Matthew 25:14-30 and Luke 19:11-27), the person who would not responsibly work was left with nothing. And the part that is the most offensive in today's political climate is that Jesus took what little the irresponsible servant had and gave it to the person who had the most. Jesus Christ is not politically correct. But He is correct. Until I can see God's value for increase and heartily say "amen" to His decision in this story, I do not have His mind.

VIPs—Jesus models how to interact with important people. He never changed who He was or His message to appeal to famous people. He lived unmoved and unimpressed with position and title, yet served them like He would any other. He understands that all promotion comes from Him. Yet He made room for a religious leader named Nicodemus, who was afraid of the opinion of His peers, to come to Him in the night. This is a brilliant example of the Son of God standing firm in His laying down what it meant to follow Him, yet He had grace for those who had a heart to obey but lacked the courage needed in that moment. At the death of Christ it was Nicodemus who brought the spices for His burial and put the body of Jesus in his own tomb. The courageous death of Jesus imparted a courageous life for Nicodemus.

Satan—He didn't chase the devil. But He dealt with him when he got in the way of His redemptive purposes and lifestyle. He also never lived in reaction to the powers of darkness, but instead He lived in response to the Father. The devil loves the attention that many believers give him.

Religious Leaders—Jesus had little toleration for religious leaders who used their position for personal gain.

Yet He welcomed honest conversation and interaction from those who were true to their call and displayed the necessary humility and hunger. He also acknowledged when they had great faith or wisdom in their conversations. (See Mark 12:34.)

Political Issues—He knew the hot political issues of His day and could have addressed any of them at any time. He taught on His Kingdom, which always aimed at the heart. Those teachings contained the answers needed to deal with the issues of His day and ours. He chose to provide instruction on how to thrive in less than ideal circumstances. For example, slavery: Jesus worked for all to become free. The Father was the one who created the concept of Jubilee, so that even in Old Testament times those who ended up in slavery due to poor decisions would always have the hope of becoming free. In the meantime, He helped slaves know how better to live in their tragic setting. Early in US history, people assumed His silence on this issue meant He supported slavery. Nothing could be further from the truth. He came to set people of every race free. Period. And while slavery is now illegal, many slaves still exist—to debt, bitterness, addictions—and in many parts of the world there is sex trafficking and, in some nations, actual slavery.

Sinners—Jesus showed us how to interact with people who were recognized by society as sinners. He spent time with them, but He didn't live the lifestyle of sin they were known for. He was called *the Friend of sinners*. The religious leaders of the day criticized Jesus quite heavily because of the people He interacted with. It should be noted that sinners loved to be with Jesus but rarely like to be with us. And tragically, the believers that sinners often do like to be with do so because they practice the same compromising lifestyles that the unbeliever practices. Jesus was the holiest person ever to walk this planet. As such, He was still welcomed by sinners, which tells me that people have an ingrained appetite for true holiness. I'd like to suggest that love— real love—has that effect on people. It is what everyone is hungry for.

> *Jesus ruined every funeral He attended, including His own.*

Angels—Jesus modeled the value of angels in His conversations and in His teaching. He was ministered to by angels in a place of fatigue and had them ascend and descend upon Him throughout His earthly life. But they were never worshiped or made the focal point of the life of a believer. I like to put it this way: angels are never to be worshiped—but neither are they to be ignored.

Government—His approach to government is fascinating and right. We are to give Caesar what belongs to him in taxes, as governments serve a purpose in representing God in protecting and empowering people. I'm glad that Jesus walked the earth in a bad political season; otherwise, we would be able to say our allegiance to governments is only due when they are righteous.

Funerals—Jesus ruined every funeral He attended, including His own. His approach to death is noteworthy. Why did Jesus raise the dead? Because not everyone dies in God's timing. Therefore, it is important we take on His approach to this very serious subject and not so quickly assume that every death was in God's plan and purpose. The Bible says it is appointed for us to die (see Hebrews 9:27). *When* is the only question at hand, and we have a role in how that plays out.

That Which Brings Us Together

All the prophets spoke of Jesus' coming. They served us well by announcing both His coming and the impact of His coming. The prophet Jeremiah gives us one of the most wonderful passages in this regard. Here is the impact:

> *"Therefore they shall come and sing in the height of Zion,*
>
> ***Streaming to the goodness of the Lord***
>
> *For wheat and new wine and oil,*
>
> *For the young of the flock and the herd;*
>
> *Their souls shall be like a well-watered garden,*
>
> *And they shall sorrow no more at all.*
>
> *Then shall the virgin rejoice in the dance,*
>
> *And the young men and the old, together;*
>
> *For I will turn their mourning to joy,*
>
> *Will comfort them,*
>
> *And make them rejoice rather than sorrow.*

> *"I will satiate the soul of the priests with abundance,*
>
> *And **My people shall be satisfied with My goodness**," says the Lord* (Jeremiah 31:12-14 NKJV).

This passage excites me. The picture is so clear. The people of God will stream, flow like a river in one direction, to the goodness of the Lord. The Kingdom of God is the land of His goodness. This is the great discovery. His goodness is in itself an inexhaustible source of joy and delight. The word *satiate* means "to fill to the full." So here we see it: the priests—that is, every New Testament believer (see 1 Peter 2:9)—are filled to the fullest, to a place of delight and complete satisfaction with the goodness of the Lord.

God's Goodness Is Always Evident

God sprinkled the entire Old Testament with evidence of His goodness, profoundly visible for those hungry enough to see it. He was setting the stage for the greatest revelation of all time—Jesus Christ. Jesus is a revelation of the heart and nature of God the Father. One of my favorite New Testament Scriptures on this theme speaks of how God revealed His heart throughout Old Testament times. It is one that deeply moves me, as it shows the heart of God reaching out to people before there is a relationship. It's found in Acts 14:17 (NKJV): *"Nevertheless He did not leave Himself without witness, in that He did good, gave us rain from heaven and fruitful seasons, filling our hearts with food and gladness."*

Before we even come to know God as our Father, He is doing things to fill our hearts with gladness. That is amazing. It's His calling card. This simple approach by God is what He calls *leaving Himself a witness*. Consider this: a witness to an event of any kind is someone who speaks not from hearsay, but from personal experience, from firsthand knowledge of the subject at hand. When God leaves Himself a witness, He is drawing each person to Himself to experience His favor. His desire is for that favor to awaken a longing in their hearts to know Him as their Father. He will not force Himself upon us, as He continues to work to protect one of the most glorious parts of His creation—the free will of humankind. Yet, in His longing for us,

He draws us to Himself through the blessings that can only come from a good Father.

In representing the Father in the Sermon on the Mount, Jesus made a startling statement, following it with an even more startling question: *"If you then, being evil, know how to give good gifts to your children, how much more will your Father who is in heaven give good things to those who ask Him!"* (Matthew 7:11 NKJV). Jesus acknowledges that it is possible for evil people to do good things. But He uses that as the backdrop for an amazing revelation of the nature and heart of the Father. All of us have sinned. And even in a sinful state we are capable of doing good things for our children.

On the other hand, God is the ultimate in perfect holiness and purity. He has never sinned in action, not even in thought or intent. Jesus challenges us to use our imagination to consider the goodness of His Father as compared to ours by asking, *"How much more will your Father who is in heaven give good things to those who ask Him!"* That moves me deeply. The question, "How much more?" is the one left echoing in my heart. And it has to do with a Father not merely meeting basic needs.

That is a given. He knows what we need before we ask and has promised to care for us. (See Matthew 6:8.) This time He is speaking of a Father who meets the cries and, more importantly, the dreams of the heart of His children. The word used for good things is fascinating. It means *that which produces benefits and implies attractiveness and excellence.*

As you can see, this is far beyond meeting basic needs. He is a loving Father, not the caretaker of an orphanage, guaranteeing us three meals a day and a cot to sleep on at night. His approach to us is based entirely on who He is—perfect in holiness, beauty, wisdom, understanding, and love. He has big-time love for all His children that is demonstrated by His giving gifts to them according to who they are and what's in their hearts. Remember, this is preceded by a question that is eternal and without limits—*How much more?*

Bless What He Blesses

One of the things that is sometimes hard to get used to is that God loves to bless both the righteous and the unrighteous. We celebrate the times when God gives a brilliant insight to a believer. Whether that insight cures a disease, or makes possible a new invention that will serve mankind well, or brings peace between two nations in conflict through His beloved peacemaker, it's something that we are all encouraged to hear about. I believe He is affirming the gifts and callings of this servant of the Lord and is using him or her in a profound way to increase the witness of His heart for people. But it must also be acknowledged that He sometimes chooses to do the same through unbelievers who at times are extremely wicked in lifestyle and even purpose. What is God doing by giving such treasure to the wicked? Leaving a witness.

One of the more frightening examples of this in Scripture is with Herod. He gave a speech to a crowd that was not inclined to idolize him yet kept shouting, *"The voice of a god and not of a man!' Then immediately an angel of the Lord struck him, because he did not give glory to God. And he was eaten by worms and died"* (Acts 12:22-23 NKJV). Consider this: he was killed because he did not give glory to God for his ability to impact the crowd profoundly with his speech. That implies that it was the grace of God that was upon him to speak something meaningful to the people. God anointed him. This is especially hard for the Church to recognize in this hour.

Political tensions are high, and if someone doesn't boldly confess a born-again experience in Christ, and then model it in a Mother Teresa-type fashion, the Church is likely to criticize and reject that individual. It's become hard for us to recognize the anointing that rests upon people who sometimes are not believers. This is especially true if that person doesn't meet our personal criteria for a leader. If the person has made moral and political blunders in his past, there's little chance the Church will see the hand of God upon him for His appointed time. Seeing through the eyes of a perfect Father, who always has redemptive purposes in all He does, is necessary in this hour.

The bottom line is, the anointing of God can rest upon ungodly people for divine purposes. We see that again with Caiaphas, the high priest, in John 11:49-52. He prophesied about the crucifixion of Christ and the effects it would have on the nation of Israel. He declared the word of the Lord, not from his relationship with God, but because of his position. There are times when God rests upon a life entirely for the person—the calling card of blessing. And sometimes that grace is upon the person for the sake of the people he serves or influences, as was the case with Caiaphas. It's our job to recognize it if we intend to see the full effect of His calling card upon society.

Jesus taught us in the Sermon on the Mount, *"But I tell you, **love your enemies** and pray for those who persecute you, **that you may be children of your Father in heaven**. He causes his sun to rise on the evil and the good, and **sends rain on the righteous and the unrighteous"*** (Matthew 5:44-45 NIV). God's approach is to show favor and blessing to all. If we want to emulate this wonderful Father, proving that we are truly sons of our Father, we must love those who have not earned it. This is the heart of God. It proves to be a vital part of understanding how this Kingdom works. If He chooses to give favor to the most wicked among us, who am I to choose to condemn and reject? I must bless what He blesses, knowing He is leaving His mark upon the hearts of people in a way that He chooses, the way that He knows works best.

> *I will not sacrifice my knowledge of the goodness of God on the altar of human reasoning so that I can have an explanation for why a tragedy has happened.*

I love to hear stories of people who have had unusual favor or blessing come into their lives that changed everything for the rest of their lives. Oftentimes these types of experiences will make the headlines. Tears often come to my eyes when I hear of how God has left a mark of favor on a person's life long before he could earn it. These stories almost always include the unusual coincidence or what some might call a twist of fate. In reality, they are God leaving His calling card, the one that shouts His goodness, so that He might be known as the Father of all that is right in the world. In this way, He summons people into an eternal destiny of delight, if they care enough to slow down, recognize the source, saying "yes" to the only One with the right to rule their lives. And rule He does—right into the greatest freedoms imaginable.

God is God, and He will always do as He pleases. He is not subject to us and never owes us an explanation for anything, although He freely gives Himself to us over and over again. It's not as though my description of His goodness puts us in a position of control or judgment. On the contrary. All that I have written to this point is simply to declare that the cornerstone of all theology is the goodness of God. For me that means that no matter what happens, the one thing I don't question is His goodness. I may never understand how or why something happens. I will not sacrifice my knowledge of the goodness of God on the altar of human reasoning so that I can have an explanation for why a tragedy has happened. But one thing is for sure: He is good—and He is always better than I think.

Chapter 3

It's Not His Fault

Why, then, did God give them free will? Because free will, though it makes evil possible, is also the only thing that makes possible any love or goodness or joy worth having.

— C.S. Lewis, *Mere Christianity*

God is usually blamed for the evils that exist in the world because if He is God, He can remove any problem quite easily because He is big and powerful. But to rid the world of sin and its consequences would require something extremely dramatic—removing all sinners. And apart from being born again, how many of us would be left? C.S. Lewis once made a statement that has helped me quite a bit throughout the years—*"once the author steps on the stage, the play is over."* He can fix it all in a moment. But when He does, time stops, eternity begins, and the final line has been drawn in the sand. His answer would be quite painful. His patience, which we see in full operation right now, is so that we can gather as many into the family as possible. His longsuffering is beyond all of our abilities to comprehend and comes at great personal cost.

Fixing this world's problems through a "military invasion of Heaven" is not the answer we want. For then He enforces His will over humankind, destroying the greatest of all creations called the free will. In doing so He would then forfeit the chance to have a people of divine purpose. He chose instead an invasion of love, where the hearts of people are conquered by one who sacrifices fully for their well-being. As a result, we now have a Gospel of power that solves the issues at hand quite well, enabling us to bring that same message to them that changed us forever. We now just need people who believe it, live it, and will risk all to display it.

But to rid the world of sin and its consequences would require something extremely dramatic — removing all sinners. And apart from being born again, how many of us would be left?

Jesus displayed the heart of His Father perfectly in every possible situation. It didn't matter whether it was disease, tormenting demons, storms, mothers with dead children, crowds with nothing to eat, or one of the numerous other calamities recorded in the gospels. Each situation became an opportunity to reveal what the God of the universe was really like. Time and time again we are left awestruck when He is manifested as the Father we would all dream of having if we had the ability to dream in that measure. Was this display of miracles a temporary exhibition of His kindness? Many think so. For them, it was God becoming manifest in that way until the cannon of Scriptures was completed. If that weren't so sad, that idea would be laughable.

I'm so thankful for the Scriptures, the absolute Word of God. The Word of God is given for our instruction. In receiving it, we become equipped, empowered, and directed to a lifestyle that displays and fulfills the will of God on earth. It is this same Word of God that reveals Jesus as the will of God. In fact,

Jesus is the Word of God made flesh (see John 1:14), the perfect revelation of the will of God. How can it be acceptable to be devoted to the Word of God (the Bible) and not the Word of God (the person)? Jesus healed on the Sabbath because to the Father people were more important than how the religious leaders interpreted the rules. Some seem to think He has gone back to prioritizing religious leaders' interpretations of the rules, where misguided instruction speaks louder than the voice of compassion reaching out to the people in need. People are still His treasure, found in the field He purchased. The Kingdom Now was and is His answer. Love requires the display of His answers now.

Jesus was the fulfillment of an ongoing revelation of the heart of the Father. This revelation only increases from season to season. It's the principle given to us from Isaiah 9:7 (NASB): *"There will be no end to the increase of His government or of peace."* It only increases—goes forward. The concept of ongoing forward motion is repeated in 2 Corinthians 3:18: "from glory to glory." The point is, God takes us forward in an ever-increasing revelation. It never declines or goes back to inferior standards, especially those of the Old Testament.

Once the demands of the Old were met (in and by Jesus), the New came into prominence permanently. Once the real has become manifest (i.e., Jesus, the Lamb of God), we never go back to the symbolic (sacrificing sheep). Once the Kingdom has become manifest, there's no going back. If Jesus opened up the revelation of the Father through miracles, signs, and wonders, why would He then return to the inferior? He didn't. We did. And that's the point. To make sure we'd never forget the standard He set, Jesus stated the impossible: *"Very truly I tell you, whoever believes in me will do the works I have been doing, and they will do even greater things than these, because I am going to the Father"* (John 14:12 NIV). Forward motion—that's the plan of God. No retreat. And no excuses.

> *Everything in our account in Christ is beyond our wildest dreams. We can't make a withdrawal if we don't know what exists.*

What's in Your Wallet?

I can die of starvation with a million dollars in the bank. If I don't make withdrawals from what's in my account, my wealth is no better than a dream, principle, or fantasy. Everything in our account in Christ is beyond our wildest dreams. We can't make a withdrawal if we don't know what exists. Jesus models the mere beginning of what's in our account. The promises of His Word give us even greater insight into this superior reality. It's time to see what Jesus has so we can see what Jesus gave us. Here's the bottom line—He gave us everything that belongs to Him. And the Father gave Him everything! Look at it here in John 16:14-15 (NKJV), speaking of the work of the Holy Spirit—*"He will glorify Me, for He will take of what is Mine and declare it to you. All things that the Father has are Mine. Therefore I said that He will take of Mine and declare it to you."*

This really is an amazing passage of Scripture, one for which we bear great responsibility. The Holy Spirit releases what Jesus alone possesses into our accounts through declaration. Every time He speaks to us, He transfers the eternal resources of Jesus to our account, enabling us to complete our assignment: *"Heal the sick, cleanse the lepers, raise the dead, cast out demons. Freely you have received, freely give. …Go therefore and make disciples of all the nations, baptizing them in the name of*

the Father and of the Son and of the Holy Spirit, teach-
ing them to observe all things that I have commanded
you; and lo, I am with you always, even to the end of
the age" (Matthew 10:8; 28:19-20 NKJV). Notice it says
for the disciples to teach their converts all that Jesus
taught them. That ***must*** include the instruction to
heal the sick, cast out devils, etc. There was never to
be a discrepancy between how we live today and His
initial standard.

When Jesus worked in miracles, was He merely cre-
ating an appetite in us to be in Heaven for eternity?
Heaven should always remain something we are pas-
sionate about. It was Jesus who taught us how to pray,
"On earth as it is in heaven" (see Matthew 6:10 NKJV).
Yes, eternity is important. But going to Heaven is
not my responsibility. He will get me there, entirely
by His grace. My job is very specific and extremely
important—bring Heaven to earth through prayer and
obedience. Please notice that when Jesus declared the
Kingdom was at hand, He displayed it by giving life,
breaking the powers of darkness, and restoring broken
lives, hearts, and homes. He told us to pick up the same
message. Why should we expect a different outcome?

Many years ago, I read a wonderful book entitled *Kingdom Now, But Not Yet*, written by Tommy Reid, an amazing pastor and apostolic leader from Buffalo, New York. He was one of the main speakers at a conference in Portland, Oregon, I attended in the eighties. I was powerfully impacted by his teaching and then by his book. Both the title and content spoke to me deeply. I had never heard the phrase before that he used as the title of his book. It had a great impact on me because, while we live with the obvious reality of the "not yet," he introduced me to more of the "now" part of the Kingdom I had not been aware of in the measure God intended.

I realize that this is probably a personal frustration, but most of the time I cringe when I hear that phrase being used today. The reason is that I almost always hear it used to describe what we can't have now, instead of announcing what God has made available for us in this great day we live in. It's become an excuse instead of an invitation. That being said, we do live in both realities—the Kingdom is now and is to come more fully in the future. But realizing that there were generations before us that had greater breakthroughs than we've seen in our lifetime should help us recognize that there is more. Much more, designed for right now. I remind you, the increase of His government (manifestation of His rule/Kingdom) never ends! Today should always be greater than yesterday.

The Will of God

The great Bible teacher Bob Mumford wrote a wonderful book entitled *The King and You*.[1] It was here I learned something about the will of God that has helped me immensely. There are two different words used in the original language of the New Testament for the word will, referring in this case to the will of God. One is the word *boulema*, and the other is *thelema*. *Boulema* refers to what is established and fixed in the will of God. That "will" will happen regardless of who believes it, or who opposes it. The return of Christ falls into that category of the *will of God*.

The word *thelema* is quite different in that it refers to God's desires and wishes. For example, *"God is not willing that any should perish"* (2 Peter 3:9), and yet people are perishing. This realm of God's will is dependent upon people's response to God's heart—both the person perishing, and the people who have been sent by God to carry the good news of the Kingdom to the ends of the earth. We have an impact on this part of God's will being accomplished.

This is huge. God has desires that may or may not be fulfilled. Make no mistake. He has the power to make anything happen that He wants to happen. But He has the heart to work with the process of the development of His people to take responsibility and co-labor with Him. The outcome of this process is we become a people who look and live like His Son, Jesus.

The first word for the will of God, *boulema*, that I mentioned previously is referring to things that are unchangeable. For example, Jesus is coming back. You can vote *yes, no,* or *I don't care*. It matters not. We don't have a role in that decision. It is put entirely in the hands of the Father, who alone determines how and when that event will happen. On the other hand, there are many things that God would like to have happen, and has made possible, but they never will be, because believers either don't believe they are the will of God anymore or are waiting for God Himself to do them. That will is represented with the word *thelema*.

I remind you of the time Jesus told the disciples to feed the multitude of thousands when they had nothing but a child's lunch. Jesus never took back His commission to do it Himself when they said they were unable to accomplish that impossible task. He still set the stage for them to see the miracle through their hands as they handed out the food. And they did. (See Mark 6:37-44.)

The will of God has been a much-debated subject, which I often find quite entertaining. It does us no good to keep the conversation in a classroom caught up in Christian theory. It has to be taken onto the streets, where the hurting people are. The will of God must be displayed by a praying people, unwilling to sit on the sidelines and see the devil continually steal, kill, and destroy, and then watch the theorist give God the credit. Masking our unbelief with a spineless theology is the great deception. This continual misrepresentation of the nature and heart of God for one another and for the world must stop. Stupidity often looks like intelligence in the absence of experience.

> *The will of God has been a much-debated subject, which I often find quite entertaining. It does us no good to keep the conversation in a classroom caught up in Christian theory. It has to be taken onto the streets, where the hurting people are.*

Who Is in Control?

One of the most common phrases used in this discussion is that "God is in control." It is true that He is the Sovereign God. He reigns over all, and everything belongs to Him. Nothing is outside of His reach or His concern. He is all-knowing and all-powerful. But is He in control? This is not a question of His ability or His power and authority. If He is, doesn't that make Him responsible for Hitler? Is brain cancer His idea? If He is in control, then we have to credit Him with disease, earthquakes, hurricanes, and all the other calamities in life. You get the point. I think it's more accurate to say He is in charge, but He is not in control. Every parent reading this should get this point quite easily.

While we are in charge of our homes, not everything that happens under our roof is necessarily our idea or is approved by us. This is an important distinction.

Vain Babbling

It has never seemed right to me to hear Christians talk about a tragedy and then say, "It must have been the will or God, or it wouldn't have happened." Or more specifically, "Isn't it tragic for such a young man to die in that car wreck, leaving his wife and small children? But we know God works in mysterious ways." Or worse yet, "We don't know why it was God's will for that child to die, but we know God has a reason." These conversations are actually quite common—they've become normal in many settings. As heartbreaking as the disaster is, the response of believers is equally appalling, in my thinking. There's the assumption that if God wanted a different outcome, He would have made it happen. That is lazy theology that somehow releases us from responsibility by shifting the blame to a God who put us in charge.

I realize that the "us in charge" is where many will have conflict with me on this subject. I'm not sure how far to take this. Reason this through for yourself, but at least consider this: Jesus gave us a model to follow. He illustrated the will of God when facing problems. He also gave us His authority to accomplish our great assignment/commission successfully, which included teaching all future followers of Jesus the things that they were taught and modeled by Jesus Himself. He followed that with the instruction to make sure all followers would be clothed with power—the Holy Spirit.

The Holy Spirit is the resurrection power of Jesus. He made the same power available for every believer that was in the life of Jesus Christ, the Son of God, the Son of Man. Then Jesus returned to the Father, saying that we would see greater works than He did. (See John 14:12.) Do I take the assumption too far? Perhaps. But neither Jesus nor His disciples ever modeled the above reasoning of accepting a problem as the will of God. So whom did Jesus leave behind with the same tools of authority, power, and presence to deal with the threats of crisis, tragedy, disease, and disasters that He had? Us. We may not have all the responsibility when there are threats of horrific problems headed our way, but we do have some. And it's time to find out how to use the tools we've been given, and more specifically, to find out how to cooperate with the Holy Spirit in a way that brings glory to the name of Jesus in the earth, instead of making theological excuses.

As I've already stated, God can work any situation around for His glory. He is that good. And I'm thankful. I've witnessed the most horrific things happen to people, and I've seen them turn to this Father of grace and have watched as God has healed their hearts to a place of unexplainable strength. But to credit Him as the cause of the problem because He can use it redemptively is illogical and foolish. It violates the nature of God revealed in Jesus Christ. The fruit of such confusion within the family about the nature of our Father is a world around us that is even more confused about the nature of this God we have claimed wants to save them.

God has desires, wishes, and dreams. He brought us into a relationship with Him as a part of that dream. None of us were forced into this relationship with God. Now we have a position in Christ to help bring about more of His desire by having influence on what happens and what doesn't happen on planet Earth. For example, consider this very simple illustration. We carry the message of salvation. This message must be preached in all the world. If we send preachers of this message to one nation, but refuse to send any to another, there will be many times the amount of converts in the nation we chose to serve with the Gospel. Does it mean that God willed the others to miss out on eternal life? No. We did. That was our choice. God is *"not willing that any should perish but that all should come to repentance"* (2 Peter 3:9). What is God's will in this passage? That no one would perish in their sins, but that all would come to repentance. That is the will of God. Is it happening? No. Is it His fault? No. Does that mean that He is lacking the ability to bring about His desire? No. He made it possible for all to come to Christ. He gave us an example to follow in Jesus. He made us sinless through the blood of Jesus. He then commissioned us by Jesus. Then He empowered us with the same power that Jesus had in His earthly ministry. He made it possible for the will of God to be done on earth as it is in Heaven. The catalyst of that becoming reality is a people who pray—relentlessly pray—what He told us to pray: *"on earth as it is in heaven"* (see Matthew 6:10).

Let me give an example of this mystery. One of the great stories in John took place at the pool of Bethesda. I've been to the remains of that pool in Israel. And while it's not one that gathers great crowds, it is in some ways my favorite site in all of Israel. God seems to stir my heart there more than most every other site. Here is the story:

> *Now there is in Jerusalem by the Sheep Gate a pool, which is called in Hebrew, Bethesda, having five porches. In these lay a great multitude of sick people, blind, lame, paralyzed, waiting for the moving of the water. For an angel went down at a certain time into the pool and stirred up the water; then whoever stepped in first, after the stirring of the water, was made well of whatever disease he had. Now a certain man was there who had an infirmity thirty-eight years. When Jesus saw him lying there, and knew that he already had been in that condition a long time, He said to him, "Do you want to be made well?" The sick man answered Him, "Sir, I have no man to put me into the*

pool when the water is stirred up; but while I am coming, another steps down before me." Jesus said to him, "Rise, take up your bed and walk." And immediately the man was made well, took up his bed, and walked (John 5:2-9 NKJV).

This is such a beautiful story of a man without hope being touched by the compassion of Jesus. Jesus came to him representing the heavenly Father. It's priceless. If this story were to happen today, there would be initial excitement by some. But the newspaper columnists, the TV anchors, the theologians, pastors, and teachers would be interviewing the people that were around the pool that weren't healed. I'm told there easily could have been up to one thousand people or more gathered around that pool, hoping for their chance at a miracle by getting into the pool after the angel stirred the water. The interview would go something like this: "How did it feel to have Jesus walk past you to heal someone else?"

Some would use that platform to warn people of the danger of getting their hopes up, as the camera sweeps across the crowd of lame and diseased people. Many of those who represent the Church would then come to the conclusion that while this one act may have been from God, it is rather obvious evidence that it is not God's will to heal everyone. Why? Instead of trying to show us what God could do, He was trying to show us what one man could do who had no sin and was completely empowered by the Holy Spirit. If we're that concerned about this pool surrounded by sick people, Go! *"Go into all the world..."* (Mark 16:15 NKJV).

This will of God is not complicated. Jesus is the will of God. He points to a perfect Father. And that Father has great dreams and desires for each of us. We are in His heart of dreams. And those dreams are for both now and eternity. Taking the time to consider Him and think according to His heart and His nature will have a dramatic effect on what we see and experience during our lifetime. We owe it to everyone around us to consider Him as He is—a good and perfect Father.

Note

1. Bob Mumford, *The King and You* (Ada, MI: Revell Publishing, 1974).

Chapter 4

Disarming Hell Through Thanksgiving

Thanksgiving keeps us sane and alive.

When you were born again, the desire to please God and do His will became part of your nature. You don't have to work it up; it comes naturally. What many believers don't know is that God did not put that desire in us and then make His will something so obscure that we couldn't discover and accomplish it. The will of God instinctively becomes the will of believers through intimate relationship with Jesus Christ.

The will of God is not complicated. Many young people ask me to pray for them saying, "I just want to know what God's will is for my life." I often tell them that I already know what God's will is. It is found in the Lord's Prayer: *"Your will be done on earth as it is in heaven*" (Matthew 6:10). God's will is simply for Heaven's reality to become earth's reality.

Our Role in Fulfilling "As It Is In Heaven"

We are God's delegated authority. As such, our obedience plays an important role in seeing the will of God accomplished on the earth. In First Thessalonians 5:16-18 (NKJV), Paul instructs us to: *"Rejoice always, pray without ceasing, in everything give thanks; for this is the will of God in Christ Jesus for you."* Two things in this statement stand out. First of all, the will of God is not merely focused on whether we become a doctor or a teacher or whether we're supposed to have tuna or peanut butter for lunch. It is focused on what we do to position our heart in relationship to God at all times, in all circumstances.

Second, rejoicing, praying, and thanksgiving are all acts of our will that—particularly in times of difficulty, weakness, and uncertainty—require faith. They are activities that draw our focus to Heaven so we can agree with what is true, no matter what we feel or perceive with our physical senses and emotions. And since our agreement is what attracts the strength and reality of Heaven into our lives and circumstances, it makes sense that these activities fulfill the will of God expressed in the Lord's Prayer—on earth as it is in Heaven. The transformation of the heart is the first step in bringing heaven to earth.

Because rejoicing, prayer, and thanksgiving attract Heaven, they are vital tools for strengthening ourselves in the Lord. You'll notice that all of them are meant to be continuously ongoing in our lives. They're not reserved for crises or holidays. They are a lifestyle—as are all the tools that we use to minister to ourselves. A big reason for this is that in the midst of crisis and difficulty, it is usually hard if not impossible to sit down and reason out how we should respond. Difficulty has a way of exposing the degree to which our lives and minds have been truly transformed by a heavenly perspective for certain responses to be habitual. The things we practice as a lifestyle equip us for difficulties.

The Lord has taught me to rejoice and pray and to be thankful—which all bring us strength. Thanksgiving agrees with Heaven by acknowledging the truth that our lives are a gift from God, and that He is sovereign over all. God is extravagantly generous, and the life He has given us to experience on this planet is not a life of survival, but of abundance and blessing. But unless we properly recognize what we've been given, we won't be able to experience that life. That's the reality of receiving a gift. If we don't understand what we've been given, we won't understand its purpose and be able to experience its benefit.

Imagine Christmas morning. You've spent the last few months shopping and picking out unique gifts for each of your family members that show your intimate knowledge of their interests and desires. You have spared no expense to get gifts of the highest quality that will be both enjoyable and beneficial to each person. But when your family comes to the Christmas tree, one person completely ignores the presents. Another person opens your gift, but starts using it for something other than what it was made for. Still another just holds the gift, and refuses to unwrap it. And to make matters worse, none of them even acknowledge that their gifts are from you. Can you see how these responses are not only foolish, but are deeply harmful to the relationship?

Sadly, this is how many Christians respond to God's gifts, particularly the gifts of the Spirit. So many people fail to receive what the Lord has offered them because they don't understand what the gifts are or how to use them. They say ridiculous things like, "Well, tongues is the least of the gifts, so I don't need to pursue it." If my children said this about one of the presents I had put under the tree for them, I'd be very upset. I'd say, "This is yours! I don't care how small you think it is. I bought it with you in mind, and I don't give cheap gifts. If you'll just open it, I'll show you what it is and how to use it." Such a rejection of gifts is absolute arrogance.

Thankfulness carries an attitude of humility. Thanksgiving is the only proper way to receive what God has given us because it honors our relationship with Him by expressing trust in His goodness, even if we don't yet understand what we've received. God gives us *"every good and perfect gift"* for two primary reasons (see James 1:17). He gives to make us prosper so we can succeed in life, and He gives to demonstrate His love as an invitation to relationship. When we practice thanksgiving as a lifestyle, we recognize that the gifts we have received from the Lord came with these purposes. Thanksgiving sets us on a course to know God in relationship and discover the reasons why He made us.

The Great Price of Little Thanks

When God tells us to give Him thanks, He's not insinuating that He gives in order to get something from us. He doesn't manipulate us with His gifts. He wants us to thank Him because thankfulness acknowledges the truth about our lives. And when we agree with the truth, then the truth sets us free to see and manifest the greatness that He has put in us as the ones He has made in His image. When we withhold thanks from God, we actually cut ourselves off from who we are. This is what Paul explains in Romans 1:18-21 (NKJV):

> *For the wrath of God is revealed from heaven against all ungodliness and unrighteousness of men, who suppress the truth in unrighteousness…so that they are without excuse, because, although they knew God, they did not glorify Him as God, nor were thankful, but became*

futile in their thoughts, and their foolish hearts were darkened.

Paul is basically saying that God has not kept who He is a secret. Knowing God is not hard. It's actually the most obvious thing in the world. All you have to do is glorify Him as God and be thankful. This response, because it agrees with the truth, gives you open access to the vast treasures of the knowledge of God. But without that response, your thoughts become futile and your heart is darkened. *Futile* means "purposeless." When we fail to sustain the response of thanksgiving for everything in our lives, our thinking is cut off from our purpose in God. When we lose sight of our purpose, we will inevitably make choices that are outside of God's intentions for our lives, and this can only be destructive because it works against His design for us.

A dark heart is a heart unable to perceive spiritual reality. It is unmoved by the desires and affections of the Lord, and therefore cannot respond to His invitation to relationship, which is the source of life. As Paul goes on to explain in Romans chapter 1, a dark heart perverts our desires and leads us into all kinds of sin that degrades our identity and relationships. The most perverted sins known to humankind came about through a door left open because of the absence of thankfulness.

The Purifying Nature of Thankfulness

Since thanksgiving keeps us sane and alive by connecting us to the source of our life and purpose, it makes sense that Paul instructs us to give thanks "in everything" (1 Thessalonians 5:18 NKJV).

Thanksgiving keeps us sane and alive.

But there is a specific dimension of thanksgiving that is particularly powerful in times of difficulty and adversity. We find this principle in Paul's first letter to Timothy.

> *Now the Spirit expressly says that in latter times some will depart from the faith, giving heed to deceiving spirits and doctrines of demons... commanding to abstain from foods which God created to be received with thanksgiving by those who believe and know the truth. For every*

creature of God is good, and nothing is to be refused if it is received with thanksgiving; for it is sanctified by the word of God and prayer (1 Timothy 4:1-5 NKJV).

Food was one of the biggest "disputable matters" that the early Church struggled with, particularly regarding the issue of eating food offered to idols. Jewish and Gentile believers alike feared that this food was defiled by having been dedicated to demonic spirits. False teachers of the time preyed upon this superstition and caused all kinds of bondage and division.

Interestingly, in the passage from 1 Timothy 4, Paul doesn't debunk the superstition and say that dedicating food to idols is powerless. He simply says that combining thanksgiving with the Word and prayer is powerful enough to deauthorize that dedication and create a stronger one—a dedication to the Lord. He is saying thanksgiving sanctifies whatever it touches.

Sanctification is a significant subject throughout Scripture. In the Old Testament it was primarily associated with the specific rituals God prescribed for setting aside various instruments, vessels, and pieces of furniture for priestly use in the Tabernacle of Moses, and later the Temple of Solomon. After a goldsmith had finished fashioning a bowl for use in the sacrifices, for example, it would be sprinkled with blood from the altar. From that point on, it would never be used for anything but priestly service in the Temple. It was completely set apart for God—sanctified.

In the New Testament, believers are sanctified by the blood of Jesus and set apart for God. This sanctification is even more powerful, because we do not merely become vessels that He can use to accomplish His purposes. The very process by which His life, power and love flow through us is the process that transforms us into His likeness. We become like the One with whom we are set apart.

When Paul says that thanksgiving sanctifies unclean food, he is saying that it sets it apart for God and His purposes. Thanksgiving actually changes the very nature of the food into something holy. This truth extends beyond unclean food. It extends to every situation in your life in which you find other powers at work besides the power of God. It's vital to remember that not everything that happens in life is His will. He didn't cause the crisis a nation or individual may be facing. He actually can't give things that are not good because He doesn't have them. Someone can only give what he has.

God only gives good gifts, because He is good, and has only good gifts to give. So giving thanks in everything does not mean saying that the adversity came from God. But giving thanks in the midst of an adverse situation, a difficulty intended to undermine your faith and destroy you, enables you to take hold of that situation and set it apart to God and His purposes.

When you give thanks, the weapon the enemy meant to use to dislodge you from your divine purpose is put into your hands and becomes the very thing that brings you more fully into that purpose. Jesus declared that He sends us out with the same assignment the Father gave to Him—to destroy the works of the devil (see 1 John 3:8). Thanksgiving accomplishes the divine justice of the Kingdom, where the enemy is destroyed by the very thing he intended to use for our destruction.

Just knowing that we can participate in destroying the enemy's purposes should alone move us to give thanks!

Releasing Justice

One of the clearest examples of divine justice in Scripture is found in the Book of Esther: the story of Haman, who was hung on the very gallows he built to destroy Mordecai. Later, this justice was made even more complete when Mordecai assumed Haman's position in the king's court. The wonderful thing about this story is that Mordecai didn't have to bring justice himself. He simply kept his focus on his duty to the heathen king and to his people. This is the nature of warfare in the Kingdom. We don't battle by focusing on the devil. We keep our focus on the King and His Kingdom, and the devil cannot help but be unseated by God's ever-increasing government released through our lives, which illustrates another reason why thanksgiving is powerful in times of adversity.

Psalm 100:4 (NKJV) says that we *"Enter into His gates with thanksgiving."* Thanksgiving brings us into the manifest presence of God and connects us with what He is doing and saying in the midst of our circumstances.

Thanksgiving helps to establish our focus on Him so that our awareness shifts from earthly reality to heavenly reality—which we must do in order to release the strength of Heaven into our circumstances.

Awareness of God

I have purposed to try to live in such a way that nothing ever gets bigger than my consciousness of God's presence. Sometimes conflict can be as simple as bad news on TV. If it starts to weigh on my heart and grow bigger than my awareness of God, I consciously turn my affection toward Him to become more aware of His presence. If that doesn't work, *I turn off the TV or leave the room to redirect my focus until* **my awareness of Him is bigger than what weighs heavily on my heart**. I can't just know in my head that He's bigger; I have to have my entire being in a position where I am aware of His presence and expect His world to invade my life and circumstances. If I don't sustain this expectation, I will expect other forces to be the prime movers in my life and will begin to live defensively instead of offensively.

When I stay close to the presence of God through thanksgiving, I not only become aware of His absolute ability to invade the impossible, I sense His radical love and delight in me! As I give thanks for the good gifts He's put in my life, I present convincing evidence that He is my Father, He is for me, and His opinion pretty much cancels out all the others. The wonderful thing is that when we simply begin to give thanks, even when it seems difficult to remember one answered prayer, it isn't too long before our focus on the good in our lives creates an opening for the Lord's joy. And it's *the joy of the Lord is our strength.*

> *If we don't sustain this expectation, other forces will be the prime movers in our lives and we will live defensively instead of offensively.*

I believe that James was talking about giving thanks when he said to count it all joy *in trial, because giving thanks usually includes taking an inventory of God's gifts in your life. Do the math! If you want to discover the ability of thankfulness to bring you strength in difficulty, you need to keep counting these things until you come to the conclusion—it's time to rejoice! It becomes really hard to stay depressed about your circumstances when you're filled with the awareness of the love and goodness of God that surrounds and infuses your life.*

There is a level of life we can reach where we practice thanksgiving as a lifestyle—a place where we remember our answered prayers. When difficulty comes along, we have a huge inventory of blessings instantly accessible to bring us into His presence as well as the joy and delight He has over us. That is a reality far greater than any accusation, crisis, or conflict that could come our way. When we learn to live in this realm, nothing can deflect us from our purpose. We even make the enemy help us get it done. From Heaven's perspective, it is reasonable to give thanks *"in everything"!*

About the Author

Bill Johnson is a fifth-generation pastor with a rich heritage in the Holy Spirit. Bill and his wife, Beni, are the senior leaders of Bethel Church in Redding, California, and serve a growing number of churches that cross denominational lines, demonstrate power, and partner for revival. Bill's vision is for all believers to experience God's presence and operate in the miraculous—as expressed in his bestselling books *When Heaven Invades Earth* and *Hosting the Presence*. The Johnsons have three children and ten grandchildren.

Made in the USA
Columbia, SC
02 June 2022